W9-AYN-860

INTRODUCTION BY

Gayle King

EDITED BY PAIGE KENDIG

INSPIRING WORDS FROM INSPIRING PEOPLE

Simon & Schuster Paperbacks

NEW YORK LONDON TORONTO SYDNEY NEW DELHI

Simon & Schuster Paperbacks
An Imprint of Simon & Schuster, Inc.
1230 Avenue of the Americas
New York, NY 10020

First Simon & Schuster trade paperback edition April 2019

SIMON & SCHUSTER PAPERBACKS and colophon are registered trademarks of Simon & Schuster, Inc.

For information about special discounts for bulk purchases, please contact Simon & Schuster Special Sales at 1-866-506-1949 or business@simonandschuster.com.

The Simon & Schuster Speakers Bureau can bring authors to your live event. For more information or to book an event contact the Simon & Schuster Speakers Bureau at 1-866-248-3049 or visit our website at www.simonspeakers.com.

Interior design by Ruth Lee-Mui

Manufactured in the United States of America

1 3 5 7 9 10 8 6 4 2

Library of Congress Cataloging-in-Publication Data is available for the original hardcover edition.

ISBN 978-1-9821-0208-1
ISBN 978-1-9821-0209-8 (pbk)
ISBN 978-1-9821-0210-4 (ebook)

Contents

CONTENTS

CONTENTS

Note to Self

Introduction

It's funny the things that stay with you. I was in third or maybe fourth grade, studying the presidents, when a boy named Wayne Viviano decided to share his latest off-the-mark epiphany with me: "If it weren't for Abraham Lincoln," he said, "you'd be my slave!"

I remember feeling embarrassed, looking around the room to see if anyone else had heard him and wondering if other kids felt the same way. I remember rushing home after school to ask my mother if Wayne was telling the truth. My mom reassured me: "Wayne Viviano doesn't know what he's talking about," she said.

So if I could send that skinny little nine-year-old girl with the braided pigtails and the happy smile a message from the woman she had grown up to be, what is it I would tell her?

That's the premise of our "Note to Self" Emmy-nominated series on *CBS This Morning*. We asked visionaries, entertainers, politicians, humanitarians, athletes—even a Muppet—what they'd want to tell their younger selves, and we filmed every man, woman, and frog as they read their answers.

The real question is this: How would *you* answer if you could write the younger you a letter? What advice, comfort, insight would you choose to include? Would you let your seventh-grade self know that sometimes insecurity comes across as mean? Would you tell your twentysomething self that not getting the job you thought you really wanted was actually a blessing in disguise? Would you share your hard-earned wisdom that it's dangerous to see your worth through somebody else's eyes? Maybe you would choose to concentrate on how to manage life's big relationships. Imagine being able to send word that marriage gets complicated and that sometimes the decision to stick it out—or to leave—is the best one you will make in life. Or maybe you could warn your younger self that the parents you thought were invincible will make some giant mistakes. I don't know about you, but there were a few times when the only thing my younger self wanted to hear was very simple: You are going to get through this with your body and soul intact. That's also the healing message of our segment, and of this book.

Reading these letters is just about as thought-provoking, wrenching, relatable, funny, powerful, and comforting as going back in time and delivering a Note to Self message of your own.

That's partly because each person in this collection speaks from a place of hard-won enlightenment. They are people who've been tested. Many have gone through unimaginable loss; many have triumphed in ways nobody believed possible. All have faith, resilience, and a mighty heart. Vice President

Joe Biden is a man who has learned that when you get knocked down, you've got to get back up and start looking hard—*really* hard—for the small kindnesses, the tender mercies, and the genuine good that still exists. Jimmy Greene writes of channeling grief into music after losing his beautiful six-year-old daughter, Ana Grace, on a sunny December morning in 2012 when she became one of the twenty-six people massacred at Sandy Hook Elementary School.

Jane Fonda is another story. She wants you to understand that despite people constantly telling you to how to live, you will only be happy being your true self. Here is what she writes: "You'll come to find that you have to be perfect—meaning thin and pretty and appealing and certainly not angry, a quote unquote 'good girl'—if you want to be loved. Living inauthentically will lead you to various addictions that will dominate much of your life."

Astronaut Peggy Whitson found her most profound happiness while away from the planet, but it took her some real earthly work to get there. As she tells her younger self:

"It will take several years of raising and selling chickens to earn enough money to take your own flying lessons. But just remember, learning to fly with that chicken money will be the first step toward a higher purpose. Because one day, you will become a real space explorer." And after living six hundred and sixty-five days in space, Whitson also found that she was far more capable than she ever realized—she even managed to write her Note to Self while in orbit! There's a lot to be said for staying true to yourself and your dreams, and Oprah Winfrey says exactly that when she writes to her younger self about "moving with the flow of life."

It's not easy to pick a favorite Note to Self, but I keep going back to Ryan O'Callaghan's letter again and again. No one would ever look at this burly, tobacco-chewing NFL lineman and suspect that he felt broken and alone and so ashamed of being gay that he'd even begun planning his suicide.

Ryan's Note to Self had those of us at the *CBS* table reaching for the tissues, but I'm hoping it has some of you reaching for a pen and writing a note that speaks to the person you were in the past in a way that nourishes you, motivates you, and teaches you something about who you used to be and who you are today.

Let the feelings flow . . .

Gayle

OPRAH

TV host, actress, producer, and philanthropist Oprah Winfrey is best known for hosting her own talk show, The Oprah Winfrey Show, *from 1986–2011. It remains the highest-rated daytime talk show in history. Among other accolades, she has received the Presidential Medal of Freedom, a Kennedy Center Honors, and thirty-nine Daytime Emmy Awards.*

Dear Beautiful Brown-Skinned Girl,

And I use the word *beautiful* because I know that's never a word you would call yourself. I look into your eyes and see the light and hope of myself.

In this photo you are just about to turn twenty, posing outside the television station where you were recently hired as a reporter. You look calm, happy, but I know how scared you are. If I could say anything to you it would be, *Relax, it's going to be OK, girl.*

You're proud of yourself for getting this job, but also

uncertain. Uncertain that you'll be able to manage all of your college classes because you're still just a sophomore and work a full day's job doing the news. Even so, your biggest concern right now? How to manage your love life with Bubba. Yes, you are dating someone named Bubba.

On this day you've brought him to the station to see where you work, hoping he'll be proud. He seems less than impressed. The truth is, you can't see it, but he's intimidated. You don't know this, though, because you see yourself only through his eyes. A lesson you'll have to learn again and again and again: to see yourself with your own eyes, and to love yourself through your own heart.

You've spent too many days and years trying to please other people and be what they wanted you to be. I understand how and why that happened now. You will have to learn that the wounds of your past—being raped at nine years old; molested from the time you were ten through fourteen; getting whipped as a young girl by people who said they loved you, because you "stepped out of place," and not even being allowed to show any anger or crying afterward—that damaged your self-esteem. If only now you knew how much. Yet through it all, you managed to hold on to a belief in God and, more important, you know—God's belief in you. That, my dear, will be your single greatest gift: knowing that there is a power greater than yourself and trusting that force to guide you.

The trajectory of your life changed the day you answered that call from Chris Clark, the news director at WLAC-TV. Your response was ignited by the words of your then-favorite Bible verse, remember, Philippians 3:14. You used to say it all the time: "I press toward the mark for the prize of the high calling of God." Knowing there is a high calling is what will sustain and fulfill you.

From where I sit now viewing your journey, there really are very few regrets. Which means a life well lived. Even then you understood that success was a process and that moving with the flow of life and not against it would be your greatest achievement.

You have made me proud.

Oprah

KERMIT THE FROG

Kermit the Frog is a Muppet created by the late Jim Henson. He was first introduced to audiences in 1955.

Dear Kermit the Tadpole,

This may come as a shock to you, but . . . I miss my tail. Oh, I know how you feel.

But for now, enjoy being a tadpole, getting to spend your day with nothing to do but swim and eat flies. Savor it. Not the flies, your childhood. Because once your tail drops and you start hopping, the hopping never stops.

Oh, it will be a good kind of hopping. And the first place you'll hop is Washington, DC. You'll love it. It used to be a swamp. Still is, kind of.

But relax, you're not going into politics. You're going there to break into television on a show called *Sam and Friends*. If you think it's not easy being green, wait till you try being black and white . . . and working in drag. But that's who you are: you'll do just about anything to make your dreams come true.

Right now I know those dreams may seem impossible, but please don't give up. Dreams are here to challenge us. Always imagine the biggest possible picture of life that you can, and act in service of that picture every single day. Keeping your eye on that big picture will put you in big pictures . . . TV shows! Movies! Guest spots! You'll work with the biggest stars in the world!

And throughout your journey you'll meet fellow dreamers of every size, shape, and species: bears and pigs and penguins and rats and . . . uh, whatever. On the outside those friends may look strange, but on the inside, they're just like you. I'll warn you: these friends will make your life crazy, chaotic, and unforgettably strange. Gee, what Miss Piggy alone will do to you is worth a separate letter—and PowerPoint presentation—but I'll save that for when you're older.

But whatever craziness these friends bring . . . it's worth it. Because here's the big secret of life: if you really want to make your dreams come true . . . share them with others.

Your dream is about singing and dancing and making people happy. That's the kind of dream that gets better the more people you share it with. Your friends—and your dreams—just need someone to believe in them. That someone is you.

Before I go, there's one other thing I want to give you a heads-up about. In a few years, you're going to meet someone who will help shape your life. No, not the pig. This time I'm talking about a guy named Jim Henson. To tell you the truth, I'm still not sure what Jim did. But I can tell you this: he'll move you, he'll inspire you, he'll give you a hand whenever you need it, and he'll never leave you out on a limb.

Kermit, I envy the life you have ahead of you. You might even say I'm green with envy. Which reminds me: have a sense of humor. Life is too silly not to laugh.

It's like my friend Jim Henson said: "It's a good life, enjoy it."

I couldn't have said that better myself.

Amphibiously yours,

Kermit the Frog

RYAN O'CALLAGHAN

Ryan O'Callaghan is an openly gay former NFL player. He played offensive tackle for the New England Patriots and Kansas City Chiefs.

Hey Bud,

Happy Graduation. You just received a full-ride scholarship to Berkeley and that intimidates you. After your California high school all-star game against Florida, you realized that you don't know nearly as much about football as you could, and now it seems that life is pointing you in that direction.

And yet, you are questioning the point of pursuing football, and beyond that, you are questioning your reasons for living. You've felt discouraged and even shunned by friends and family your whole life, hearing the word "fag" out of the mouths of your loved ones and knowing that they're talking about you. You, a gay football player.

I know you think that's an oxymoron, and that's why your first goal is to make sure no one finds out. I know you are in pain. I know you are confused. I know you are battling an inner turmoil that will last another decade.

Breathe.

You're about to enter the toughest years of your life. You're going to succeed at a sport that serves as your cover. While you're at Cal, you're even going to be voted the best offensive lineman by your opposing peers. They all think you are a force to be reckoned with. They see this potential in you that you have trouble seeing in yourself.

You will make it all the way to the NFL, playing first for the New England Patriots and then for the Kansas City Chiefs. You are going to invest all of your energy and time into football so people refrain from asking your least favorite question: "Where's your girlfriend?" You are going to start chewing tobacco in order to look more straight. Don't do it. You're going to gain as much weight as possible so that people see you as unattractive. You're going to do everything in your power to make sure no one finds out that you're gay. You know that if your cover is blown, you'll lose everything. If you're gay, you're as good as dead.

You will live twenty-nine years of your life in fear. You'll keep up this facade because you think there is no alternative. You will want to escape the anxiety, to feel something other than trapped. This is why you will abuse drugs, especially painkillers. You will even spend and donate hundreds of thousands of dollars because you have no intention of needing it, because after your NFL career, you will plan to take your own life.

But you won't.

Your athletic trainer will notice your downward spiral and convince you to talk to a counselor. This will be the turning point for your whole life and give you the strength necessary to find out that people love you: your family, your friends, and your dogs.

You will realize, Ryan, that you have been scared for nothing. This is not the end. No, this is just the beginning.

You will soon feel free for the first time in your life. Heck, you might even find love with someone who understands you and your struggle.

So again, breathe. Really. Breathe. Believe it or not, it gets better for you, and soon you will want to share this newfound happiness and love with the world.

Just hang in there a little longer, buddy. One day, people will look up to you for your strength.

Ryan

VICE PRESIDENT JOE BIDEN

Joe Biden was a United States senator for thirty-six years before becoming the 47th vice president of the United States alongside President Barack Obama.

Dear Joe,

You're only twelve. Your stutter is debilitating. It embarrasses you and the bullies are vicious.

But listen to Mom when she says, "Bravery resides in every heart—and yours is fierce and clear." Listen to Dad when he says, "Joey, when you get knocked down, get up, get up."

Because if you listen, you'll summon the bravery to overcome the stutter and you'll learn to stand up to bullies.

You'll learn from Dad, who moved the family to look for work, that a job is about a lot more than a paycheck—it's about your dignity; it's about respect.

And that's why you'll follow your heart and serve your community, your state, and your country.

An intolerance for the abuse of power will drive you to stand up for civil rights.

And because you listened, you'll live a life fully consistent with what you were taught by Mom and Dad and your faith.

That you should say what you mean and mean what you say. Leading by the power of example will define you, and one day, you'll find yourself forging a relationship with a Jesuit Pope who embodies that universal truth.

But you'll also learn early—and later—in your life that reality has a way of intruding.

One day you're on top of the world, only to be brought down in a flash with a profound loss and a grief that leaves a black hole in your heart, questions of faith in your soul, and an anger beyond rage.

That's when you'll have to dig deep and live what Mom taught you—that out of everything terrible that happens, something good will come if you look hard enough. You'll hold on with faith and pure grit.

You'll be blessed with a love that will anchor you as deeply as your faith.

Your bond with your children and your grandchildren will be your redemption.

Because of a family grounded in unconditional love and loyalty, and the compassion of friends and strangers—you'll get up, you'll keep going, and you'll give back.

You'll realize that countless people have suffered equally or more, but with much less support and much less reason to want to get back up.

But they do, they get up.

They keep going.

And so must you.

You'll learn what it means to be an American. There is no "quit" in America.

Being there for family and friends; serving your country; building real relationships, even with people with whom you vehemently disagree—that's America. Made up of ordinary people, like you, capable of doing extraordinary things.

And one day when you graduate from law school, you'll decide to become a public defender.

In the midst of the epic struggle for civil rights, you'll be walking the streets on the east side of Wilmington, much of which has been burned to the ground after your heroes were assassinated.

Forty years later, you'll stand on a train platform of Wilmington overlooking the east side.

Wilmington and the nation will no longer be in flames but awaiting a new ripple of hope.

You'll be waiting for a young black man, inspired by the dream of a King, coming from Philadelphia to pick you up and take you on a 124-mile trip to Washington to be sworn in as president and vice president of the United States of America.

Together, you'll prove that change is hard but necessary;

progress is never easy but always possible; and things do get better on our march toward a more perfect union.

That's the history of the journey of America.

And believe it or not, because you listened to Mom and Dad, you'll help write it.

Keep the faith, Joey.

Joe

KESHA

Kesha Rose Sebert is a Grammy-nominated American singer, songwriter, and rapper from Los Angeles whose songs have reached the top of pop charts.

Dear Kesha,

At this very moment you may be wondering if it was really a good idea to drop out of high school and move to LA with nothing but your grandpa's Lincoln Town Car and a demo tape.

I've got good news and I've got bad news, and I know you're a tad impatient, so I'll start with the good news. You made it! And thank God, because the best plan B we ever came up with was waitressing and we will soon find out that is not really our forte.

The bad news is, you nearly killed yourself on the road to success, fueled by fear of failure, crippling anxiety, and insecurity. You will become severely bulimic and anorexic, and the worse your disease gets, the more praise you will get from some people in your industry. And this will really, really mess with your head. But when you're trying to live up to an unrealistic expectation, it's never going to be good enough, no matter what you do.

Right now you're killing it on Myspace, but beware, because the internet will get way less innocent real fast. Save yourself some anxiety and a few years' worth of therapy and just skip the comment section. Skip it all together. It's a breeding ground for negativity and hate. And don't let people scare and shame you into changing the things about yourself that make you unique and interesting. Those are the qualities that will make your life so magical. That bad girl, I-don't-give-a-s*** attitude, it'll work for a while, and you will get a dollar sign tattooed on your hand that will probably last forever. But the truth is, you don't need to put on an act. You can just be Kesha Rose Sebert, and guess what? Apparently that's good enough.

People will listen to your music and come to your shows as long as the art is honest and good and you're just being yourself. You're still in a society that worships photoshopped supermodels. We all still feel the pressure to look like them because that's a symptom of a society that emphasizes all the wrong things, and this will be an everyday struggle. You must be strong, 'cause over time you will gain confidence and you will learn that words and art do matter.

You will meet kids who tell you that they struggle with many of the same things you've struggled with, or more. And they're gonna tell you that your music helped save their life, and that will change you. You're gonna learn that art can heal people.

I know you are very inspired by Bob Dylan and he's your favorite. Bob Dylan is one of the reasons you play music, and one day you're gonna meet him and you're going to weep hysterical, happy tears at the thought of it.

One day you're gonna write a song called "Rainbow" and you're gonna be really proud of it, because there is light and beauty after the storm, no matter how hard things get. You're going to write this song so you remember to make it through. You're going to remind yourself to love yourself and if you have truth in your heart, there will always be a rainbow at the end of the storm.

Kesha

DALE EARNHARDT JR.

Dale Earnhardt Jr. is a retired professional stock car driver and team owner. He is the son of NASCAR Hall of Fame driver Dale Earnhardt Sr., who died in a crash during the final lap of the 2001 Daytona 500.

To Sixteen-Year-Old Dale Jr.,

Now, writing this letter to you is going to force me to think pretty deeply about my life, and you know thinking deeply was never one of your favorite activities. You always did and always will shoot for the C on your report card; anything more than that is always going to be a surprise to you, right?

You just got your driver's license, your heart belongs to no one, and you're going to spend a lot of nights in the bed of your S10 pickup truck out in the field staring up at the stars, worrying about your future. Your father's accomplishments on the racetrack already cast a pretty heavy shadow over your existence. He's going to accomplish more in the years to come and your fear of living anonymously and forgotten—that's going to grow.

You don't have much of a connection to your mother; your efforts in that regard are disappointing. In the future she is going to become a consistent and prominent figure in your life, but you shouldn't waste the years in between. Because her love is the truly unconditional kind. You shouldn't take it for granted.

Living under your father's roof doesn't bridge the incredible gap between you guys. In due time, you will enjoy the most incredible relationship with him. One afternoon after an accident, you're going to go home thinking your career is over. And then bustin' in through the door comes your dad, and he's wondering what you're doing sitting on your butt feeling sorry for yourself. And you are going to go out on the back porch and sit down and have a two-hour conversation that is the most influential conversation you'll ever have with him. He is going to finally assure you of what lies ahead. It's not the end of your career like you thought, it's just the beginning of a very, very long, incredible journey.

You'll share laughs and triumphs at his side. It'll be in your best interest that when these times come, you get everything out of them that you possibly can. I mean, when it is you and him in that moment, you live it to the fullest.

Now, you want to be a race car driver, so let's talk about the racing. As I look back on it as a whole, starting out from go-karts all the way to Cup today, it's going to feel clunky and impromptu, and is going to be lacking in successes. But fortunately for you, every weekend there will be another race.

With that said, you're going to be so deathly frightened of potential failure that you're not going to realize just how much fun you're having. You're going to win a lot of races, and as painfully shy as you are, you'll overcome and accomplish in arenas not just limited to driving cars. You're going to meet presidents. You're going to guest on late-night shows. I mean, it's incredible—but it's true.

That's not too bad for an oil mechanic. Yes, you are going

to change oil for a few years—and it's not as bad as it sounds.

Overall, you just need to be more sure of yourself. You're going to do great things, man. You're going to have an awesome life. You have a great heart and it's going to stay with you throughout. So don't be so timid and worrisome about the future that you can't enjoy the present. You're there, worried about me here. You just need to have some fun, man. Jump in that S10, go down to Concord and cruise the strip. Because you're going to be here soon enough.

Dale

DR. RUTH

Dr. Ruth Westheimer is a German-born Jewish immigrant to the United States who became an author, radio, and TV host specializing in relationship and sex advice.

Dear Ruth,

You're ten years old. You're on a train. You've just watched your mother and grandmother run alongside that train desperately waving good-bye as it pulled out of the station at Frankfurt am Main. Your father has already been taken by the Nazis. You're bewildered, lonely, and sad, but you have no idea how much sadder you'll be when it becomes evident that you will never see any of your family members again . . . that you are an orphan.

Trains always take their passengers on a journey, but for most passengers, there is a round-trip ticket in their pocket. For you, Karola Ruth Siegel, you're being launched into a journey that will never end. The tug of home, the desire to see your father, mother, and grandparents even one more time will never really fade.

Of course, there were six million other Jews such as yourself, who not only weren't able to go home, but whose lives were snuffed out for no other reason than they were born Jewish. So while you will bemoan your fate during the six years you will spend at the Jewish boarding school in Heiden, a school that for the German Jews became an orphanage, one day you will realize how very, very lucky you are. And later, coming to the realization of how fortune smiled down on you even as it was ripping your heart out, you'll know that you have to squeeze more out of life than other people, because you are living not just for yourself but for your entire family.

I could never begin to explain to you the changes that are going to take place in your life. Even your names are going to be inverted, so that you'll be known as Ruth instead of Karola. You'll also feel bad about never growing to the height that most people do, but you'll overcome all that and succeed in making a new family who will be more dear to you than you could possibly imagine, because they'll be living proof that Hitler failed at wiping out your family.

And so as I sit here writing to you while on the stage of a theater where a show about your life is being performed nightly, all I can say to you is to try to have as much courage as you can. You'll need it, but your bravery will be well rewarded.

Oh yes, one last thing. You know that time you made a ladder out of a chair and some books to reach that locked cabinet where Mom and Dad kept that book about sex? Give yourself a pat on the back for that.

Ruth

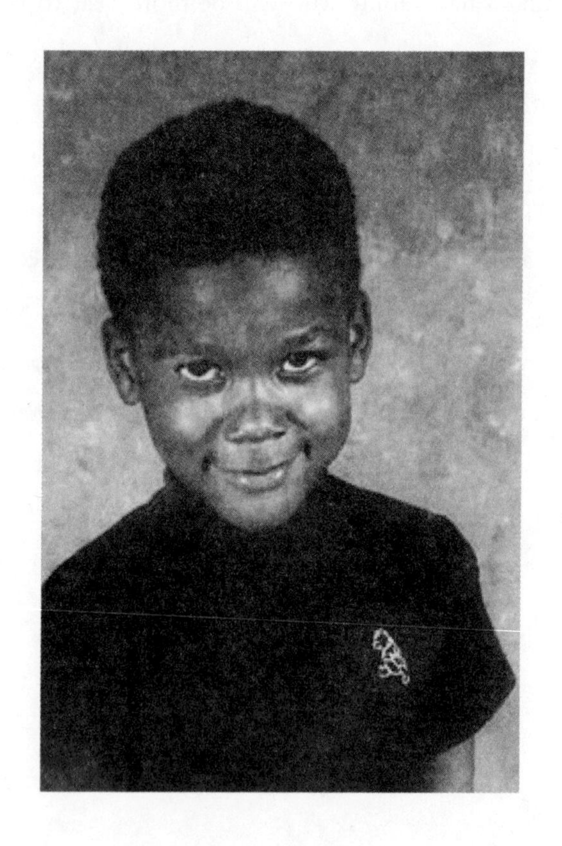

TYLER PERRY

Tyler Perry is an American actor, writer, director, and producer of film and TV.

Dear Child of God,

In this picture I see you trying to smile, but that smirk is all you could muster. I know that you're having it really hard right now, and you spend a lot of time using your imagination, seeing yourself running free in the park, away from all the pain.

In the reflection of your very sad eyes I see the hurt of watching your mother be belittled and beaten. I see the pain of your own beatings and the barrage of insults that you suffer and endure every day. I feel the horror of the hands of the molesters who are trying to rob you of who you are.

As I search your young face for any sign of myself, believe it or not, I'm able to smile . . . because just behind all of that darkness I see hope. You've got some kind of faith in God, little one.

I know that you don't know this right now, but who you become is being shaped inside of every one of those experiences. The good, the bad, and yes, even the ugly ones. They all are going to work together for your good.

I know that's hard for you to understand right now, but I promise you, you are going to get to a point where you use all of it, every bit of it, to make yourself better, and stronger . . . and you're gonna use it in your work to uplift and encourage and inspire millions of people. It all works together for your good. It's all in God's hands.

You're so uncertain about a lot of things. Right now the most important thing to you as a man-child is growing up to be able to take care of your mother. Don't worry about that . . . you do. And she is happier than she could ever be as you grow up.

You're uncertain about becoming an adult, because every friend that you have is either in jail or has been murdered.

People are dying all around you, and you don't think you're going to live to see thirty years old . . . but you do. Not only do you live, you thrive.

You have a lot of challenges. A lot of things are trying to shake you, but there's one thing that can't be shaken and that's your faith in God. Even now at your very young age, there's a still small voice that speaks to you. You don't know what it is but looking back on it, I know that it is the voice of God. There's no other way to explain how you're able to know what you know, how you're able to understand what you understand at that age, how you're able to navigate through those turbulent tough times. Yes, that is the voice of God. Like when you're told that you're nothing by many people . . . that voice tells you you're something. Or when that teacher tells you you'll never make it because you're poor and you're black and you're from the ghetto, that voice says, "She's wrong. That's not true." You'll remember that moment because it changes your life. You're gonna be all right.

I just want you to know, you beat everybody who beat

you. And all that time you spent trying to make your mom smile by imitating her and dancing and laughing, keep that up, boy . . . it pays off big-time.

Thank you for living so that I could thrive.

Thank you.

Tyler

FRANK GEHRY

Frank Gehry is an American architect whose buildings dot skylines across the world.

Dear Frank,

I guess the most important advice I would give to you is to keep a copy of *Don Quixote* and *Alice in Wonderland* at your bedside for your entire life! The world is an upside-down place and you have to make your own logic out of the insanity. That can get pretty scary pretty quickly, but don't be afraid of yourself, of who you are. Believe in yourself and be curious. Follow that curiosity every day in everything that you do, even when the world tells you that you are nuts. Create your own logic and follow it to where it leads you and try to enjoy the ride.

You were born Frank Owen Goldberg in Canada in a climate of anti-Semitism. You will experience this first-hand at restaurants with signs reading NO JEWS ALLOWED. Go in anyway. You will be the only Jewish kid in the elementary school and will get beat up regularly for killing Christ. You can't change this, but recognize that there are people who will beat you up for your entire life for the stupidest reasons. You can't change who you are, so stay your course even in the face of extreme idiocy.

In your family, your mother and father will be tough on you. Your father will be worried that you are a dreamer and that you won't amount to much. You mother will compare you to the children of her friends and, in her eyes, you will always be lacking in some regard. You will feel misunderstood and hurt but understand that this is their version of love. They had many of their own obstacles to overcome. Watching them struggle through these hardships, survive, pick themselves up, and get to work in spite of their misfortunes will give you a model of courage that you will carry with you your entire life as you face larger and more complicated crises.

Despite your financial situation, you will have access to

lectures and cultural institutions that will feed your curiosity. Your mother will introduce you to the Art Gallery of Ontario, where you will develop your lifelong love of painting and sculpture. She will take you to classical music concerts that will ignite your soul. You will not understand how it fits into your life or how it fits into your father's conception of your life, but you know that art will be your salvation. Keep looking at it and search it out. Seek out others who have the same curiosity and don't listen to anyone who tells you otherwise—they are simply not having as much fun with life.

You will figure out how art plays into your life in college. Your ceramics teacher at night school, Glen Lukens, will open up the world to you. He will see a real spark in you when he introduces you to architecture. He will even pay for you to take a course in architecture. His mentorship will change your life forever. You will find the profession that makes sense to you and gives you a sense of personal pride.

You will be tested again and again. You will have a teacher

tell you, "This ain't for you, Frank. Find another profession." Get pissed off and ignore him and vow to prove him wrong. When you run into him later in life, he will say, "I know, I know—I was wrong."

Once you find your passion for architecture, work your tail off to understand and build expertise on every facet of the profession. Listen to your professional practice teacher, who will tell you that no matter what you do, however big or small, make it the best thing that you can, because you will be judged on everything you do. Make sure that everything you design and build adheres to your highest standards. Push back on people who try to dilute this mission and partner with the people who support it. Be parental with clients—they are expecting your best work. Never presume anything; understand their point of view—the work is always a partnership. Take every crisis as an opportunity to do better work.

Create buildings and places that engage people. It doesn't mean pandering to historical models of the past. It means finding a way in the present to engage in creating humanistic environments. Certain styles of art and architecture are about the denial of humanity. Remember that architecture is inclusive, not exclusive. It is meant to support and elevate feelings. Question everything, be curious forever, and never forget that life is about people. So make buildings for people and always use the natural light—it's free!

Frank

JANE FONDA

Jane Fonda is a two-time Academy Award–winning actress, author, and political activist.

Dear Jane,

What you don't realize now is that your life will be a *big* wide circle passing through many dark periods when you will see no future for yourself, when you won't know who you are, and you won't feel anyone could possibly love you.

Right now you want to be a boy, preferably a Native American boy living in the wilderness and passing through it silently, invisibly, with stealth.

You will be sexually molested at seven, just as your mother was as a child. When you are twelve, your mother will take her life, and the bravery and spunk of your earlier years will seem to fall by the wayside.

You'll come to feel that you have to be perfect—meaning

thin and pretty and appealing and certainly not angry, a quote unquote "good girl"—if you want to be loved. Living inauthentically will lead you to various addictions that will dominate much of your life and energy.

Your parents are both self-involved, so you will grow up not really knowing what love feels like. What will come to pass is that, through a lot of hard work, you will realize that your parents did the best they could. You will learn to remember them with compassion and become your own person.

I wish I could explain to you that the painful things that will make your life challenging and get you in trouble are the things that will ultimately make you strong and compassionate.

Your biggest strength will be that you won't give up, you won't become cynical, you will become an activist. You will discover that doing this will give your life a meaning you don't think possible. It will be your rent for life.

You are a late bloomer, so it won't happen quickly, but your ability to be honest with yourself, your desire to make sense of it all, to learn from your mistakes, will permit you to blossom in life. A woman with courage, imagination, and resilience.

As I read this I am about to turn seventy-eight. And though I know you find this impossible to believe, this is the happiest I have ever been. It was all worth it, the good and the bad.

So don't give up. I'm proud of you, because you will never settle for less than you think you can attain.

Love,

Jane

JOHN LEWIS

Congressman John Lewis is a civil rights activist whose actions helped end legalized racial segregation. He has served Georgia as a US representative since 1987.

Young John Lewis,

You are so full of passion. In your lifetime, you will be arrested forty-five times in your mission to help redeem the soul of America.

In 1956, when you were only sixteen years old, you and some of your brothers and sisters and first cousins went down to the public library trying to get library cards, trying to check out some books, and you were told by the librarian that the library is for whites only, and not for coloreds.

I say to you now, when you see something that is not right, not fair, not just, you have a moral obligation to continue to speak up, to speak out.

You became so inspired by Dr. King and Rosa Parks that you got involved in the civil rights movement. Something touched you and suggested that you write a letter to Dr. King. You didn't tell your teachers; you didn't tell your mother and your father. Dr. King wrote you back and invited you to come to Montgomery.

In the meantime, you have been admitted to a little school in Nashville, Tennessee. And it was there that you got involved in the sit-ins.

You'd be sitting there in an orderly, peaceful, nonviolent fashion and someone would come up and spit on you, or put a lighted cigarette down your back, pour hot water, hot coffee, hot chocolate on you.

You got arrested the first time, and you felt so free. You felt liberated. You felt like you had crossed over.

You probably would never believe it, but the "Boy from Troy," as Dr. King used to call you, will become the embodiment of nonviolence in America.

Two years after you speak at the March on Washington,

you will see the face of death while leading the march for voting across the Edmund Pettus Bridge in Selma.

You were beaten on that bridge. You were left bloody. You thought you were going to die. But you will make it. You will live to see your mother and father cast their first votes. You will also live to see this segregated nation we live in send an African American president and his family to the White House.

And guess what? Guess what, young John? By some divine providence, as if to send a message down through the ages, that man will be nominated on the forty-fifth anniversary of the March on Washington.

And all those signs that you saw as a little child that said WHITE MEN, COLORED MEN, WHITE WOMEN, COLORED WOMEN—those signs are gone. And the only places you will see those signs today will be in a book, in a museum, or a video.

John, thank you. For going to the library with your brothers, your sisters, and cousins. You were denied a library card;

you were sad. But one day you will be elected to the Congress. You will write a book called *Walking with the Wind* and the same library will invite you to come back for a book signing, where black and white citizens will show up. And after the book signing, they will give you a library card.

I believe as Dr. King and A. Philip Randolph and others taught you, that we're one people and it doesn't matter whether we're black, or white, Latino, Asian American, or Native American. That maybe our foremothers and our forefathers all came here in different ships, but we're all in the same boat now.

John, you understood the words of Dr. King when he said, "We must learn to live together as brothers or perish together as fools."

John

ALICE WATERS

Alice Waters is a California-based chef best known for pioneering the farm-to-table culinary movement at her restaurant Chez Panisse.

Hey you,

I bet you don't want to listen to anything I have to say. You've got such an independent streak—I know that. You don't want anyone telling you what to do. But, please, I have some important things I want to tell you.

First, don't ever lose that sense of independence. Or doubt it. It's your greatest strength. Even if the way you're seeing things feels like the loneliest place in the world—trust it. It's the greatest thing anyone of us can do, actually—trust our own instincts.

And trust your senses—especially your sense of taste. You probably aren't even aware of how sensitive you are now, but, believe me, your senses of taste and smell and sight and touch are going to be your personal treasure. Your senses will lead you to people and places that will fill your life with richness and happiness and give it meaning and depth. And, believe it or not, you will find your life's mission in helping others bring their senses alive.

And I know this sounds crazy—because you're such a picky eater and all you want to do right now is drink strawberry milkshakes and eat a grilled cheese sandwich—but you're going to start cooking and loving it! Your whole life is going to be centered around cooking! I'm not kidding. Your ways of cooking will be a revelation not only to yourself but to others as well. Have confidence in it. You will find that cooking is a way to build community when communities are beginning to fall apart around the world. You can't comprehend this now, but cooking real food will become a powerful way to bring people to the table, feed them ideas, and start a revolution.

I know you don't like getting your hands dirty yet, but you are going to become a true friend of farmers and growers—so be prepared!

Don't be afraid to work hard and realize that sometimes the smallest and the dirtiest jobs are often the most important. Don't judge what work is valid and what isn't—just jump in and do what needs doing when it needs doing! Work and pleasure will become the same thing.

Always collaborate. You are strong at some things but not everything, and others' strengths will inspire you to create something that is greater than the sum of its parts. But always remember to be grateful.

I know you'll always have this wild side of you and you'll have many adventures and romantic relationships. And that's OK—it's great, in fact. But I want you to know, so you don't worry about it, that you will be married one day and you will have a beautiful child. And having that child will not only fulfill you and give you your greatest friends in the world, but it will open up a whole new chapter late in your life, one filled with a brand-new passion—transforming public education by awakening children's senses, nourishing their minds and bodies, and teaching them the values that we need for the future of this planet.

Alice

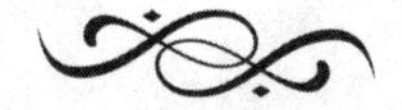

SCOTT OSTROM

Scott Ostrom served his country as a United States Marine. He was deployed to Iraq twice, and returned home with post-traumatic stress disorder.

Dear Fifteen-Year-Old Scott,

You're living with your dad in Lake Tahoe. You want nothing more than to be with your mom, stepdad, and little brother back in Florida. Mostly because your father has been such a hard-ass. It doesn't make much sense now, but he has been prepping you to function at high levels of stress and excel at the toughest job the marines has to offer.

You'll enlist seven days before our president declares war on a country you've never heard of. You will excel in boot camp, thanks to the discipline your father taught you. In Iraq, chewing tobacco, standing watch, mortar attacks, cleaning your rifle, *Cherry Magazine*, driving all night, and shaving your face all come before sleeping—get used to it, kid.

While you're there you will get a chance to fight. And it will be everything you imagined it could be. Knowing you have a distinct path to travel—dark and hard—will not be any easier because you put your own feet on it knowingly and willingly. You escape with just a few scrapes and bruises. But . . . it will leave invisible wounds you could never have imagined.

When you get home, it will feel like you lived somewhere where the volume was so loud that the silence back home feels deafening, and you'll want to scream. Some nights you will. Real sleep comes at a premium; mostly what you will get is the agitated side of half sleep—less like sleeping and more like waiting. You'll experience night sweats, harsh functionings of consciousness, drifting in and out of your head, and a corroded appetite. You will experience simple daily stressors as if they are being cut into you with a razor, and you will either become depressed or explode in a fit of vengeful rage.

Iraq made you tougher than any civilian can imagine. Keep yourself out of county jail by not proving how tough you are to frat boys, bad drivers, and sloppy drunks. Your behavior will make your family and old friends uncomfortable, so embrace your brothers, because they understand you. Once you become a marine, you'll have friends—wherever you are—right by your side.

You will soon receive the best friend a man coming home from war can have: a service dog from Puppies Behind Bars. His name is Tim and he is trained in over ninety voice commands. This may sound extraordinary, but what's really metaphysical and amazing about this animal is how he will train *you*. He will train you to be calm, have empathy, be patient, trust strangers, nurture a loving relationship, laugh with abandon, and so much more. He will be there when you need someone to lean on and wake you up from those bad sleeps of pain and rage with a kiss.

Surround yourself with people that love you and want to understand you—Tim will weed out the undesirables.

Overcoming and adapting to your new environment will set you free. Moving forward, help yourself, and when you're ready, help your brothers.

You haven't done the most important thing in your life. Dying doesn't make you a hero. Never quitting, never surrendering, and never giving up—that makes you a hero.

Scott

PIPER KERMAN

Piper Kerman was convicted of money laundering and spent a year in a women's prison. Her memoir about her experience was the inspiration behind the TV series Orange Is the New Black.

Dear Piper,

You are out there pushing yourself as hard as possible to get beyond your perceived boundaries—limitations associated with your gender, class, and age. There are certain things that "nice young women" just don't do, and you are very interested in them.

You are trying to put as much distance as possible between you and what you think is expected of you; you will go halfway around the world and do the wrong things. You just don't fully comprehend the consequences of your choices, not only for you but for others. In fact, you think your actions are inconsequential. You are mistaken. Being a badass is seriously overrated.

Stop for a moment and step outside of yourself. Notice the wider world around you and not just your hurtling trajectory through it.

When you are in trouble, your family is going to astound you with their tremendous reserves of love and unwavering support, so be a better daughter and a better sister now.

Lucky for you that you have already forged friendships that are going to last for decades. The day will come when the people who love you most will stand by you, despite all your mistakes and flaws. So forgive them theirs.

You're going to meet a man who will change your life. Yes, that's hard to believe at the moment, as you wouldn't currently touch a man with a ten-foot pole. But you're going to surprise everyone, most of all yourself, when you fall head over heels in love with him. And when your past comes back with ferocious fangs to threaten your life together, he's somehow not going to be scared, not rattled. His love is going to sustain you.

The day is going to come when you seem to lose everything. When you are sitting in a prison bunk after mail call, reading friends' letters voraciously and gratefully, you will recognize them as your lifeline. But all these people and the things they taught you are still going to be there, and that's what will get you through dark days and tight spots behind the walls of the biggest prison system in the world.

You and your choices in the world matter a great deal, and not just to you. As a very young woman it may not seem like you are powerful and have an impact on others. You do. So draw on every advantage you've been given and do the right thing and the kind thing, as often as humanly possible.

And don't be afraid to tell the truth.

Piper

CHRIS ROSATI

Chris Rosati was diagnosed with Lou Gehrig's disease, or ALS, at age thirty-nine while expecting his second child. Chris passed away from the disease in 2017.

Dear Chris,

I am happy. And I am about to die.

How I got to be both is a beautiful story, and it begins with you.

You are on your knees in a cold exam room, waiting for the doctor to tell you what you already know—that there is no cure, that you will not live to walk your girls down the aisle.

You are lost. Alone. And you are terrified.

I can barely move, typing this with my eyes. But I'm not lost. I'm damn sure not alone. Scared? Yes. Also increasingly optimistic.

Stand up. And I will tell you what you need to know about the journey from your moment to mine.

You will face a struggle even your worried mind cannot imagine. Hurt is coming. You will lose the ability to hold your children, to touch your wife's face. You will look into the souls of those you love, and you will hurt for their sadness.

Your wife will be the one who makes you believe in true love. She's beautiful and funny and she believes in you. When you lack the strength, she lifts you up. After all these years, you still count the stars that shine in her eyes.

Then there are two smile makers that are beautiful through and through. They will make you so happy. They are Empathy and Courage. They bring laughter and love, purpose and peace. They will see you at our worst. And they will make you better.

This may be hard to believe, but from all the pain, you will find your redemption.

You will focus on what you love: making people smile.

You'll discover the best way to make people happy is by

helping them make others feel happy. That can make you feel alive—even when you feel like you are dying.

And the girls, they will be okay. They will be shaped by the journey, but they won't be defined by it. They're learning that the best way to live is to give, to worry less, and when we do what we love, we can do more than we ever imagined.

ALS may kill you, but it will make them better.

So go hug the folks running down the hall. Hug, cry, scream, hurt—feel it all. But know that both despite and because of the sadness, the struggle, and the misfortune, there are moments I look around now and wonder if I might be the luckiest man on the face of the earth.

Chris

PEGGY WHITSON

Peggy Whitson is a NASA astronaut. She became the first woman to command the International Space Station, and has spent 665 days in space, more than any other American in history.

Dear Younger Me,

I've learned a few things over the years that I would like to share with the younger version of myself.

You just watched on TV as Neil Armstrong and Buzz Aldrin took the first steps on the moon. Although at the time it was an unbelievable moment in history, seeing it with your own eyes made it real and believable and achievable. It made you feel small but filled you with excitement. That moment in time planted a seed of inspiration in you. Now it's up to you to nourish that seed and grow it into more than just a dream.

Next year your dad will get his private pilot's license.

You will get your very first ride in an airplane. The exhilarating view of the cornfields from above will inspire you to fly as well. However, it will take several years of raising and selling chickens to earn enough money to take your own flying lessons. But just remember, learning to fly with that chicken money will be the first step toward a higher purpose. Because one day, you will become a real space explorer.

The year you graduate high school, NASA will select the first female astronauts. You will dream of exploration. Know that what you dream for might seem impossible, but you will be successful as long as you make your life decisions based on your own value system and not others'. So ignore the naysayers, ignore the people who say you can't become an astronaut. Instead use it as motivation.

It will be ten years of applying before ever becoming an astronaut. The rejections will be discouraging, but in your typical style you will just keep trying. All those years of anticipation will be surpassed when the solid rocket boosters ignite, and you will literally roar into space.

Seeing the Earth for the first time in orbit, you will be surprised that you never noticed the quality and texture of colors. High above Earth, you will remember what your parents taught you growing up on the farm: problems don't always have elegant or expensive solutions. Dad will teach you that #2 wire and pliers, plus a healthy attitude, can fix almost anything.

Believe it or not, you will spend more time in space than any other American astronaut and earn the nickname Space Ninja. You will grow soy beans in orbit while your father will grow soy beans on Earth. You will have the opportunity to help build the engineering marvel that is the International Space Station. You will walk in space ten times! You will find that living in space can actually become a home, in spite of tools floating away. Alien to all you know, you will adapt and you will love it.

Know that even though it is incomprehensible to you, you will be a role model. I am still struggling with this one, so you need to step up a bit earlier than I have done. I would tell you not to underestimate your abilities, but since I know you I'll just say: challenge yourself. You will learn that you are so much more capable than you might imagine or even dream.

Sincerely,
The Older You

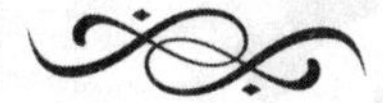

TAYA KYLE

Taya Kyle is a mother of two from Texas. Her husband, Chris Kyle, was a US Navy Seal known as the American Sniper. He was killed in 2013.

Dear Taya:

There's so much I could tell you that you're going to experience—joy beyond your wildest dreams, and a grief so terrible you'll be sure it will break you.

I wish I could keep you from the pain, but life isn't like that.

When you're in your early twenties, you'll meet a man who will change your life. His name is Chris Kyle. He'll be strong, physically and emotionally, with the gentlest voice. He'll have a tremendous smile, and a sense of humor that will match yours. The two of you will fall madly in love and decide to spend the rest of your lives together.

Chris is a United States Navy SEAL. He believes in God, Country, and Family, just as you do. He'll serve four tours in Iraq. Even so, he'll find some way of being by your side when you give birth to two children, a perfect boy and a perfect girl.

You'll be so proud of him as a father and as a war hero. But every time he leaves for deployment, it will be a challenge. Every time you say good-bye to him you'll fear the worst.

Then, finally, he'll come home. Things will seem . . . perfect. Until one day, one horrible, terrible, very long day, the worst will happen when you least expect it.

It's not going to be easy. In the end you'll reach deep inside yourself to find the strength to carry through.

Try to remember these things as you go through that journey:

You like to be independent, but you will need help. And getting help does not make you weak.

At some of the most important times in your life, you will fight against fate. You won't be able to accept that you are on a path that will eventually lead you to happiness. But trust that things will work out.

Like a lot of women, you know how important your friends are. Go to them. Hold their hands. In your moments of despair, a friend's hand on yours will get you through the worst of it.

Last, but not least, enjoy every moment you can. When the dark days come, many wonderful moments . . . those will all seem dead and empty to you. It will take practice, and even hard work, to find the joy sometimes.

Sometimes you will think you can't take it another day. But if you hang in there, one step at a time, you will be able to accomplish more than you ever imagine.

Good luck, Taya. May God bless you, always.

Taya

PRESIDENT JIMMY CARTER

Jimmy Carter was the 39th President of the United States of America.

I am writing to a twelve-year-old Jimmy Carter, although I am now ninety:

As you now live and work on a farm in South Georgia and have just reached your highest goal of learning to plow a field with two mules, I hope you will not limit the other ambitions of your life. Your mother, a registered nurse, is ignoring the strict segregation that hurts your playmates and friends, all of whom are African Americans. Always cherish your close relationship with these rural neighbors and remember, as you grow older, that this racial discrimination is a blight on both white and black people.

I know your top ambition is to go to the Naval Academy and someday serve as a submarine officer. You must always do your best and use this experience to learn about the world we live in and how a strong nation can be a champion of peace. You will see how President Harry Truman's order to abolish all racial discriminations in the military service will bring welcome changes, but it will always need to be improved.

When you return home from the navy, you must use your years as a farmer to expand your heart and mind as much as your father did, as preparation for the public service that is to come. In private life and in elective office, you should remember the advice from your schoolteacher, Miss Julia Coleman: "We must accommodate changing times and still hold to unchanging principles." These principles will best be expressed in our religious faith but even more clearly and briefly in the Universal Declaration of Human Rights, which will be written after a terrible war.

Miss Julia's words will be good advice, no matter how many challenges and disappointments you will have to face. After every setback, I hope you will reexamine the causes of your failure, reassess your own talents and abilities, and then set even higher goals if that is possible.

One of your greatest sources of happiness will be your wife, Rosalynn, and the growing family that will be coming. Stay close to all of them, bring them together whenever possible, and provide them the same help and support that your own parents gave to you.

You will get to know some great people who personify these high ideals in tangible ways. Some of them will be quite famous, and others will be known just to their own immediate neighbors. Form as close a friendship with them as possible, and learn from their example. You'll face many challenges throughout your life, but don't worry. So many people will want to help you along the way.

Jimmy

DANICA PATRICK

Danica Patrick is a professional racing driver and a pioneer for women in motorsports. She became the first woman ever to win an IndyCar race in 2008.

To Sixteen-Year-Old Danica Sue Patrick,

You've said good-bye to Mom, Dad, and your sister Brooke. It's just you alone with your thoughts now as this plane crosses the Atlantic to take you to England.

This is what you wanted to do and needed to do to further your racing career. And you're really excited about it, as any sixteen-year-old would be about a great adventure.

I don't want to dampen the mood, but frankly, you should be scared as hell.

Think about it. You've left everything you've ever known—your family and friends in Roscoe, Illinois, and Hononegah

High School—all to chase a dream that may or may not come true.

I'm not going to lie to you—the next couple of years are going to be tough. You're going to face challenges that will make you wonder if it's all worth it. A lot of people aren't ready for a girl to be a successful driver, especially in Europe.

You'll call home wondering if it's time to quit and come back to the States. But you'll press on, hoping that things will get better once again.

When you do eventually come home, you're tougher than you ever thought you could be. And you'll land a job driving for an Indy 500 winner named Bobby Rahal and another guy named David Letterman (he's on TV late at night). They'll bring you through the ranks in the States before giving you what you've always dreamed about: a full-time IndyCar ride and a chance at winning the Indianapolis 500.

Those lonely feelings you had in England a few years ago?

They will be replaced by the roar of three hundred thousand people on Memorial Day weekend when you become the first woman ever to lead the Indianapolis 500. You'll finish fourth in the race and your life will never be the same again.

You'll land on the cover of *Sports Illustrated* and do all the talk shows. It's going to be a bit overwhelming but get used to it. And get used to making history.

Just a few years after that magical day at Indianapolis, you'll make history on foreign soil; not in England, mind you, but in Japan. You'll become the first woman to ever win an IndyCar race! You'll cry tears of joy in victory lane, and then enjoy a party-like atmosphere on the plane ride across the Pacific—a little bit different than the uncertainty you're currently feeling as you cross the Atlantic.

Believe it or not, you'll become a one-name person—when the name *Danica* is mentioned, people will know exactly who it is. Kind of hard to believe, isn't it? Well, the story gets a little stranger.

You'll begin to think about NASCAR. Yes, NASCAR! You'll compete in both IndyCar and NASCAR for a bit before going full-time into stock cars. That is something that I'm sure you're thinking, *No Way! That's never going to happen!*

Once again, you'll make a bit of a splash. You'll win the pole position for the Daytona 500 and lead some laps before finishing eighth. But you'll be really excited to know that you are one of only thirteen drivers to lead both the Indy 500 and the Daytona 500. You're on a list that includes names like Foyt, Unser, and Andretti!

Throughout all this, however, you'll stay true to yourself and what you believe. Some people will hate you, despise you, even. You'll use them as motivation to become better.

You'll also gain millions of fans, especially little girls, which will blow you away. You'll wonder how they even know who you are! Make sure you take time for them. Kids are so impressionable, so make sure you take the time to look them in the eye, talk to them, sign an autograph, and pose for a picture. It will mean the world to them.

And as you navigate the tough racing world and all that comes with it, just remember what your dad always told you: "Have fun."

It's so simple but so true.

Danica

ART GARFUNKEL

Art Garfunkel is an American singer and poet, best known for his work in the folk duo Simon and Garfunkel.

My Darling, My Younger Self,

What do I know that you may value? It's what *you* know that I may have forgotten. Here are some things I do know:

Singing brings joy. Such a tickle in the throat. Singing was my silent companion as I stepped over the threshold into a room of strangers.

Then, if you can embrace the differentness of another—tightly fused in beautiful dissonance—you give power to music, to musicianship, to the partner.

Fame is a kick, the party's at your house. It helps the introvert, it pays the bills, it puts momentum into the current project at hand. I met many beautiful women through the focus of fame. I met many of my fabulously talented industry players—fine artists. The buzz was real. I took flight into the open-ended artist's realm and that was the real fun.

If you marry, as I did, you will be exasperated. Boys and girls are different. But if the difference is a challenge, it is also the grand enrichment of life. Lovers soothe each other, they dance together. They combine in the great thrill—the creation of new life. And this will start the second half of your life. Adorable children will send you two parents to heaven with a godly feeling: adoration.

As you age, you get out of your own way. You will see more clearly what your unique contribution to earth is meant to be. Mine is to be a singer. Your heart will become your center place. You will know the difference between cheap thrills and deeper satisfactions, known by its calling card—hard work.

I lost my singing voice three years ago; I don't know

how. It has been hard work to regain my sound and take to the stage again. You will need to be brave to mend out in public.

But you will never ever find the right hat!

Art

JIMMY GREENE

Jimmy Greene (jimmygreene.com) is a jazz saxophonist and music teacher based outside New York City. He lost his six-year-old daughter, Ana Grace, in the Sandy Hook Elementary School shooting. He and his wife started the Ana Grace Project (anagraceproject.org) in her memory.

Dear Jimmy,

I see you out there, young man—thirteen years old, shooting hoops on the playground all by yourself. You've always been fascinated with what the future holds for you. Well, I've got a lot to share with you, son.

I'm proud of you, Jimmy. You're probably not aware of this, but as a young black man from a broken home, the odds you'll end up in prison are greater than the odds you'll end up in graduate school. You know, your mom and stepfather work really hard to provide for you so that you can get busy dreaming big dreams. Keep dreaming, Jimmy. I know you feel a lot of pressure to excel but know that it's OK to make mistakes; it's OK to not have the right answer; it's OK to show your feelings, however ugly they might be. Listen to that voice, though, Jimmy, that voice saying you'll be a musician—because you will. Those closest to you will still love you and be there for you.

You'll soon meet a man named Jackie McLean, a legendary jazz saxophonist who will inspire you to dive headfirst into music at the Artists Collective, and fall in love with jazz. Soon thereafter, you'll meet a young flute player named Nelba. Through your mutual love of playing music, your lives will be forever joined. She's funny and smart and so talented—did I mention she's gorgeous, too? Don't ever forget the way she makes you feel. The love God has kindled in you for one another will help you through some unimaginably tough days ahead.

You're going to live out your dream, son. After school you will move from your Hartford home to the Big Apple, travel the world performing with lots of your musical heroes, and make lots of recordings, playing the saxophone. As tough as a musician's life can be, God will always make a way for you. Your faith in Him, especially in times of trouble, will give you peace beyond understanding.

You'll be blessed with two children: two beautiful, talented, loving children. They will melt your heart and make traveling so much seem less attractive. You'll move the family to Canada after accepting a full-time university position so that you can be a bigger part of Isaiah's and Ana's early years. Young man, make the most of every moment you have with those angels. Your three years in Winnipeg will be the last three years your beautiful family will remain fully intact.

You'll eventually return home—a great academic position will open up at Western Connecticut State University and you'll live much closer to your family back in Hartford and your performing career's home base, New York City. Home will never be the same, though. Ana will be ripped from you—suddenly, violently, senselessly, and without warning:

murdered in her first-grade classroom along with classmates and teachers, twenty-six in all. Your son will have made it out of that building alive, but you'll cry out to God, "Why? How could you let this happen, Lord?" You'll experience shock and trauma—you'll wonder how you'll ever go on without your baby, the one who had your cheeks and your smile.

I know you and your dad haven't spoken very often lately. But know this, young man. On the worst day of your life, your father will pull you aside and give you the most helpful piece of advice a father could give. He'll say, "Your grief is real and will be with you for a while. Grieving Ana's murder will be a long process. Even so, don't let your grief blind you to the beauty of all that you still have in your life at this moment right now, and the beauty of all God has in store for you in the future."

Despite your pain and grief, there will be beauty all around you, Jimmy. The beauty of your wife and son, the beauty and generosity of your friends and family, the love and concern shown by the jazz community, your university colleagues, our nation's president, and the tens of thousands of people from all walks of life who you will never have even met. And the music in you . . . you'll find comfort in the beautiful melodies God has planted in your head. You'll write new songs, you'll play with renewed passion, and honor your daughter's life with the music that ran through her veins, that runs through your veins too.

Your favorite Bible verse, John 16:33, reads: "In this world you will have trouble. But take heart! I have overcome the world." Keep your eyes on the Lord, Jimmy. You, too, will overcome.

Jimmy

TIM HOWARD

Tim Howard is an American soccer goalie who played for England's premier leagues for thirteen years. He was diagnosed with Tourette's syndrome in sixth grade.

Dear Tim,

What have you gone and gotten yourself into now? You are twenty-four years old and you just made a massive decision that will change everything.

The MetroStars of MLS, your hometown team that you've dreamed of playing for, to the world's richest club, Manchester United.

Oh boy, good luck with that one, kid.

I guess you are going to have to grow up fast. Lean on the words you've heard your mother say a thousand times: "To whom much is given, much is required."

Deep down in your heart you know that this will be a

learning process and it will take years for you to grow into the world-class goalkeeper you hope to become. But when Sir Alex Ferguson entrusts you to wear that famous shirt within the first two weeks of your arrival, fake it and pretend that it was your expectation all along.

One important off-the-field note: the British media will try to build you up and then tear you down. Don't believe the good or the bad. When they make ignorant, classless references to your Tourette's syndrome, remain humble and grounded no matter how hard it is.

In the coming months and years, your talent and ability will be called into question. My suggestion to you would be to form a foundation built on hard work and mental fortitude. Let there be no doubt that you're a Jersey boy and in New Jersey, only the strong survive.

There are going to be highs and lows; after all, you're a goalkeeper and that's just the nature of things.

There will be games that you'll perform heroically and that will ultimately earn you the honor of Premier League

Goalkeeper of the Year. There will also be games where you make a costly error and people will have you believe it's the end of the world.

If you hear nothing else from this conversation, please hear this—never ever lose that undying belief in yourself and your abilities that you've had since age six, when Esther Howard signed you up for the North Brunswick Township recreational soccer league.

Because here's the thing: the world has lazily decided that self-confidence and self-belief are one and the same, and I'm here to tell you unequivocally that they are dead wrong.

Your confidence will ebb and flow depending on performances and results. Your self-belief, on the other hand, will give you the necessary strength to go out every day against the odds and continue to strive for greatness.

Trust me, my boy, just wait. The lights will shine brightly on you in the years to come and I promise, you won't disappoint.

Oh, and one more thing—next time you sign for

Manchester United, don't, under any circumstances, wear a shirt-and-tie combo that are the colors of their crosstown rival, Manchester City.

Above all, enjoy the next thirteen years. It will be the time of your life.

Dream big.

Tim

CHELSEA HANDLER

Chelsea Handler is an American actress, stand-up comedian, and TV host.

Dear You,

I know you are scared being so far away from your family, in a city where you know few people and you have no money, but you were brave to move all the way across the country when you were twenty. I know you don't think of yourself as brave, but that is exactly what you are. This is the first of many big leaps in your life. Don't forget this time. You are directionless in the best possible way.

Right now you're waiting tables in a little restaurant in Santa Monica called Rosti. It is one of a dozen different restaurants that you will be fired from. You don't like people telling you what to do, and this will always be a theme for you. You do not have to take every little injustice that happens at a restaurant and make it into your battle cry. You are not Joan of Arc. Wait until you're doing something that you really care about and save your passion for that.

Don't expect immediate results with anything. Be patient. I know you hate hearing that, but seriously, be patient. Put in the time and effort and then wait for the reward. It will come. You will not wait tables forever. You will live out every moment you've dreamed about, and even more. So take your time, look around, and breathe.

Please start eating healthy now. It becomes too much to unravel later. You have to create good habits now. Stop drinking soda. Don't ever drink another soda again. Start a relationship with water. I know you don't like the taste but put something in it. Lemon.

You can still drink alcohol as much as you want, as long as you do everything else I say. You have a very healthy foundation with alcohol and I will never take that away from you.

Cigarettes are harder to quit the longer you smoke, so pick an age or a number under thirty and stop the day you turn that number. You're good at quitting things, so make sure you quit the bad things too.

Don't take a water pill, a sleeping pill, or a diet pill. They are only shortcuts, and shortcuts only work for short periods of time. And eventually you will have to face the music, and it is *not* a pretty song.

Think of every relationship as an opportunity to grow, not as a soul mate. There are soul mates everywhere in life and oftentimes they are not your lovers. The world is full of men, so look at dating realistically, and think about how you want to be remembered when you break up. Do not reach out to ex-boyfriends when you've been drinking. I don't know how to make you stop doing it but stop.

You'll be exhausted most of your life, but it will be worth it. And I'm telling you it is. Don't listen to people who tell you you're doing too much. That's who you are. Flex your grit. It's okay to burn out on something. It forces you to move on.

Enjoy the struggle of the unknown, because you will have the life you always dreamed of.

Be good to all the people that love you, and always let them know that you love them back. And don't ever listen to anyone who tells you you can't. Because you can, and you will, and you do.

Love,

You

CHRIS HERREN

Chris Herren played professional basketball for the Boston Celtics and Denver Nuggets. While playing, he struggled with substance abuse and drug addiction.

Dear Christopher,

I am writing to tell you that the path you take is a tough one, but you will survive and be very happy someday.

When I look at you I see a kind, smart, athletic boy. You come from a lineage of basketball and there are unreasonable expectations. You are programmed to be tough and win.

In high school you play in sold-out gyms, getting taunted. Wearing your name on your jersey isn't easy. The scoreboard has much more meaning than fun. As your spotlight gets brighter, you feel uncomfortable and confused, not knowing your losses are as important as the wins . . . both will teach you valuable life lessons.

At fifteen you won't understand the power of the red Solo cup full of beer and the blunt that will lead you to stronger and more dangerous drugs.

Your senior year, the country's top colleges recruit you. But you choose to stay close to home. Fall River is your safe place. Your relationship with your mom is unconditional and immense. Your father and brother offer you protection from the madness around you. Heather is your sanity and one of the best things you hang on to in your life . . . and one day she will be your wife.

At Boston College, you will be introduced to one line of cocaine, and although you promise yourself one time, that one line will be the reason you get kicked off campus and barely make it through Fresno State. That one line will last fourteen years. And although you're gifted enough to get drafted into the NBA by the Denver Nuggets, your struggles will continue chasing that one line.

At twenty-two you will spend twenty dollars on a little yellow pill called OxyContin, and that 40mg pill will turn into 1600mgs a day, and that twenty dollars will turn into a twenty-thousand-dollar-a-month drug habit. And that one little yellow pill will have you outside the Boston Garden in your Celtics uniform ten minutes before a game, waiting for your dealer. That little yellow pill will strip you of your NBA dreams and goals and you will no longer be invited back into the league. Two years later, that one little yellow pill will become a syringe that will stay in your arm for the next six years.

Christopher, addiction will follow you wherever you play. Addiction will be your toughest opponent.

As a husband and father, you will spend every dime you ever made on drugs and put your family in debt. You will feel defeated and at times suicidal. But one day please know, you will find it in you to fight back.

On August 1, 2008, your awakening begins. You are granted a day off campus from treatment to see the birth of your son. Yet again, you fail. After his birth, you walk out of the hospital and go get high. Upon returning from your relapse, your counselor tells you to pick up the phone and promise your wife you will never call her again, and to tell your three kids their dad has died in a car accident, because you don't deserve a family and you should let them live. But instead you pray for sobriety; and from that prayer on, God willing, you will stay sober.

Treatment and faith gave you sobriety. It will be your life's greatest gift. Sobriety will enable you to become the man you always wanted to be. You will find your life's purpose from your struggles and you will share your story in the hope that it may help just one person. You will be a voice for those who are sick and suffering. You will no longer have shame.

And you will live one day at a time.

Chris

JIM McGREEVEY

Jim McGreevey served as the governor of New Jersey from 2002 to 2004, when he resigned after announcing that he was "a gay American." That announcement made him the first openly gay governor in US history.

Dear Jimmy,

I'm sorry for the pain and anguish of being a homosexual. Even using that word now conjures up dark, sickly, and unhealthy images. I know you've struggled to be quote unquote "normal" in the face of the taunts from other boys, calling you a "fag" and a "homo."

You've worked so diligently to prove yourself just another kid at Boy Scouts, at church outings, on the Little League field. I remember the fear when you first went to the local public library, when you thought you were a homosexual. And how your heart was pounding as your fingers went through the card catalog to look up the word *homosexuality*. And being so deathly afraid of somebody in the next aisle seeing you look up that word. Finally, when you found the word, it was listed as a psychiatric illness; how your heart began to pound and your mind began to race.

I know the anguish that you felt when you read what the church said about homosexual love—homosexual love was an abomination, that it was worthy of eternal damnation—and how crushed you were because it was the church you so dearly loved, who hated you so deeply.

And despite your best efforts to change, to try to be straight, you could never change yourself, who you were, who you are. I tried to seek acceptance at the ballot box or with public acclimations, because I was afraid to be who I was. But it did not answer the longings of my heart. And only when it was thrust upon me in the most difficult of circumstances, then did I accept my own reality. That I am a gay American.

And so, Jimmy, while you may pace about nervously or anxiously or confused at high school dances and yes, even the disaster which is your senior prom. Not to worry. One day you will meet your life's partner, fall deeply in love unconditionally, raise wondrous children, and learn to be the happiest that your heart has ever been.

In the meantime be patient, enjoy the blessings of friendship, be at peace, and accept yourself.

Love and all good things,
Jim

DR. MAYA ANGELOU

Dr. Maya Angelou was an American poet, memoirist, and civil rights activist. Among countless other awards, she received a Pulitzer Prize and the Presidential Medal of Freedom. She passed away in 2014.

This is a letter to myself when I was about fifteen:

Dear Me, Myself then . . .

First, I know that you know how to listen. When I was eight years old I became a mute and was a mute until I was thirteen, and I thought of my whole body as an ear, so I can go into a crowd and sit still and absorb all sound. That talent or ability has lasted and served me until today, when I'm eighty-three years old.

Once you appreciate one of your blessings, one of your senses, your sense of hearing, then you begin to respect the sense of seeing and touching and tasting, you learn to respect all the senses.

Find a beautiful piece of art—if you fall in love with Van Gogh or Maltese, or John Killens; or if you fall in love with the music of Coltrane, the music of Aretha Franklin, or the music of Chopin—find some beautiful art and admire it, and realize that that was created by human beings just like you, no more human, no less. The person may have keener eyesight, a better ear; the person might have a more live body and can dance, but the person cannot be more human than you.

That is very important because that ensures you that you are a human being and nothing human can be alien to you. You will be able to go around the world, learning languages, speaking to everybody, because no one can be more human than you or nor can be less human. They can be meaner or crueler, or wetter or prettier, younger, richer, but they can't be more human than you. Remember that.

Maya

TRACY MORGAN

T*racy Morgan is a stand-up comedian and Emmy-nominated actor known best for his roles on NBC's* Saturday Night Live *and* 30 Rock.

Dear Little Tracy,

I know you're scared right now, and that's all right. Your dad just left and he was your protector. You're going to be mad at him for a long time, but try to remember he was a good man. He went away and fought for his country, but came back hooked on heroin. Your mom couldn't have him in the house. She had five kids to raise and she couldn't raise them around a drug addict. It's going to be hard, but you're going to make it.

Other people in your life are going to man up, or kid up, like your older brother, Jimmy, (I love you, Jim). I know he's handicapped and can't fight all the bullies in the neighborhood when they pick on you, but he's going to protect you in other ways. He's gonna show you how to use your brain and not your fist or a gun. Of course it's not going to be easy. To paraphrase Bette Davis, it's going to be a bumpy life.

You'll watch all the old movies, like *The Maltese Falcon, Angels with Dirty Faces,* and your favorite, *To Kill a Mockingbird.* For some reason you're drawn to these films. They'll be asking, "Why is this little black kid in the projects watching old-ass white movies starring old-ass white people?" Don't worry about them, though. You're going to do a lot of things people think are crazy because you are a little crazy, boy. There's nothing wrong with that. Listen to me. Just embrace it. It's gonna come in handy.

They're going to think you're crazy when you move in with your girlfriend named Sabina and her two sons when you're twenty-two and jobless. This woman, she's gonna be the one who's going to become your wife and gonna be the one to encourage you to get onstage and be funny. She's gonna say, "I know you funny, boy, pull the trigger."

And remember, once you're onstage making them laugh, you're on your way. No heckler can hurt you. Hey, man, you've made killers in the projects laugh, so a heckler don't mean nothing. Some drunk dude in a comedy club making fun of your propeller hat, that can't intimidate you. You won't be intimidated by nothing.

Not even auditioning for TV shows like *Saturday Night Live.*

Hey, when it comes to show business, you've seen your favorites like Eddie Murphy and Richard Pryor, George Carlin—you've seen them do it a thousand times, so it ain't gonna mean nothing to you. The only thing that can stop you, little boy, is the same thing that stopped your dad—drugs and alcohol.

It'll cost you your marriage. You'll lose a good woman but not your life. You'll sober up and you'll still be funny. Nothing's gonna stop you, not even a Walmart truck. You may not know it now, but you're strong, man. You're strong. You'll have a lot of things going for you. Second chance at love and life.

Someday you're going to be a protector of your own family. And you will never, ever leave.

Tracy

HEATHER DUCKWORTH

Heather Duckworth is a wife and mother from Tampa, Florida, who suffered the loss of one of her young triplets. Heather's note was chosen from reader submissions across the country to be a part of our collection of Notes to Selves.

Dear Younger You,

Look at you. So young and innocent! I wish I could keep you like this always.

You will marry your childhood friend, the one you have known your whole life, kissing as toddlers while your parents were stationed together in the military . . . the one who really used to annoy you. But don't worry, this will be the best decision you ever make. He will love you boldly through every peak and valley of your life.

You will be anxious to start a family. Unfortunately, the joy of your first pregnancy will turn to disappointment and sorrow when you have a miscarriage. This will be your first sting of loss, but remember to stay positive because brighter days are ahead.

A year later you will be blessed with a son. And a year after that, you will find yourself pregnant again. You will have a slight complication and fear the worst. You will nervously go to the doctor and instead get the surprise of your life: You are expecting triplets. You will cry with relief as you see three tiny heartbeats on the sonogram. After a difficult pregnancy, and feeling as big as a barn, you will give birth to three beautiful, healthy baby boys. You will love these four boys fiercely and realize your greatest gift in life is being their mother, even if they run you ragged.

Three years later, your happy world will be shattered when one of your triplets is diagnosed with cancer. Your heart will break watching Jacob suffer through treatment, but he will amaze you with his courage and fight, always with a smile, and he will make you feel brave.

In the end, your son will pass away at six years old. The

pain of his loss will be unbearable and you will learn to walk hand in hand with grief for the rest of your life. It is the price of your love. Your family and children will pull you out of the trenches of grief and you will live for Jacob and he will forever be your inspiration. For a while, you will find comfort in raising money and awareness for pediatric cancer research, helping other families facing a similar fight.

A year later, having long hoped to adopt, you will fly to Guatemala with your family to meet your baby girl. You will fall instantly in love when they place your daughter in your arms—a gift to your family in so many ways as she helps your heart heal. Her joyful spirit will be a burst of sunshine in your lives.

The years will pass quickly, and before you know it Jacob's sweet little brothers will be grown men, ready to graduate from high school. You are just so proud of these boys and all that they have overcome. But this season of life will be bittersweet, because even if the world sees them as twins, they will forever be triplets in your heart.

Remember, your life is going to be filled with the greatest joys and the deepest heartaches, but you will survive. That ache in your heart will always be there, Heather, but it will make you stronger. You will hug a little tighter, cry a little easier, and smile a little bigger because of it. And you will share Jacob's story, your faith, and your grief in hopes of helping others.

Love big and hang on to hope. You can do it!

Heather

ADAM RIPPON

Adam Rippon is an American figure skater who took home the gold at the US Figure Skating Championships in 2016 and represented the United States in the 2018 Winter Olympics in PyeongChang, South Korea.

Hi Adam,

It's me, Adam, but from the future.

You are going through a really tough time right now. You've just missed qualifying for the Olympic team for the second time in a row. You feel confused and you feel like a failure. It might not make sense right now, but this is truly one of the most important moments in your life.

Take a moment and be proud of yourself.

Do you remember being thirteen and taking the Greyhound bus from Scranton to Philadelphia every Monday morning so you could get to practice? You stayed with so many different families who made you feel like you were home when you were not. It was scary and you missed your own family very much, but your mom always told you it wasn't a sacrifice if you got to do what you love. You lived in your coach's basement for a few months because you couldn't afford to live anywhere else. Not that long ago, you had so little money that sometimes you had to choose whether you paid for groceries or paid for ice time.

You work so hard, but you are even harder on yourself. Now listen, this part is important: Stand up, walk to a mirror, look yourself straight in the eye, and tell yourself: "You are a winner." You won't see one looking back at you yet, but do this every day and you'll really start to learn what being a winner is. Being a winner is a mind-set.

You came out to your friends and family a few years ago and it made you feel so free, like you'd grown wings. Do you remember growing up in Pennsylvania, thinking that being gay was something you would never tell anyone? When you publicly come out in the next year, you will let go of what other people think of you. You will hope to give someone else what you didn't feel growing up: permission to be themselves. You will be saying: "You are worthy."

Oh, and when you wax your eyebrows, start talking about how great they look. It'll be a hit.

Over the next few years, you'll get into the best shape of your life, mentally and physically, and you will feel so in control. You're not a teenager anymore and you've embraced that you aren't going to be as thin or light as some of your competitors. You worked on perfecting yourself instead of trying to change yourself.

You will become a national champion at twenty-six and your path to the Olympics will seem clearer than ever. But exactly one year before the 2018 Olympic team selection, you will break your foot. You'll fear everything you've worked for was in vain, but don't be discouraged. You are strong, you are brave; you can take on anything.

You, Adam, will make the Olympic team and skate on Olympic ice—it'll be a moment you've been waiting for your entire life. It'll be crazy, wild, emotional, and very exciting. The world will see your character and they will embrace you for just being yourself.

You are a man now. You've challenged yourself and taken risks. You make people around you laugh, and help them like who they are. You've become the role model that you wished you'd had as a kid. You will look in the mirror and you will see someone you like. You will look in the mirror and finally see a winner looking back at you.

Now go out and conquer the world!

Adam

FRANÇOIS CLEMMONS

François Clemmons is an actor, singer, and playwright known best for his appearances as Officer Clemmons on PBS's long-running television series Mister Rogers' Neighborhood.

My Dear Little Buttercup,

Yes, that's what we all used to call you. Sweet Little Buttercup. One day, if you stay focused, folks will know who you are and they won't tease you about being sweet. But for a while, they will tease you about that and singing, and wanting to play the piano and dancing and playing with jacks.

You're going to have many experiences as a little black boy growing up, particularly because you like being with the girls. And so you find yourself constantly feeling like an outsider. For whatever reason you don't want to do what the other boys are doing. You will discover that you are who you are and it cannot be prayed away.

I know that you've only seen two or three shows on television that feature someone who looks like you. But believe it or not, you will make history.

You must get to Pittsburgh. That's your appointment. Because something is going to happen to you that you've been longing for all your life. And when you meet this man, something about him is going to draw you in a way that nobody else ever drew you and pulled you. And he's going to love your singing. He's going to encourage you.

He'll change your name and call you Officer Clemmons and anoint you in your role as a "helper" on his television program, *Mister Rogers' Neighborhood.*

Growing up, you have a slightly different view of what police officers represent in your community, but your heart will open when Fred explains the positive influence that you can have for young children.

One day you will go on to college and continue to sing so that you can travel all around the world and touch the lives of many people. When you give yourself, Buttercup, folks will have a taste of that sweet life and begin to believe in themselves again. They'll know that love does exist and that there's much more that all of us can do when we choose to do it together.

François

TAMMY DUCKWORTH

US Senator Tammy Duckworth of Illinois was among the first army women to fly combat missions during Operation Iraqi Freedom, where she suffered the loss of both her legs. In 2018 she became the first senator ever to give birth while in office.

Dear Tammy,

I know you're busy focusing on acing that test or winning that next track medal, but I want you to take a step back. You'll achieve more than you ever imagined—and succeed beyond your wildest dreams—but it won't be because you were smarter, stronger, or faster than anyone else.

No matter how hard you try—and you will tear yourself up inside trying—you never will achieve that 4.0 GPA and you'll never be that high school track star that you and your parents wanted you to be. But you'll learn that perfection isn't what matters. It's how you respond to hardship and failure that defines you.

You'll see it in your daddy's eyes when his failure to prepare, make tough decisions, or set his ego aside leads to years of struggle for your family. You'll be hungry, relying on food stamps to feed yourselves. You'll be nearly homeless, having lost almost everything that's important to you. But you'll see how your family works to recover. Your family will work harder than you've ever had to before and harder than you will ever have to again. You'll come out tougher, but also more humble. You'll learn that gratitude is essential, and you'll learn how to survive a tough time—which is good, because you're going to need that skill again.

You'll join the army, and you will have two very different lives. Your first will be on a path toward a happy life and happy family, with achievements in the military and a chance to travel and see the world. But that wonderful life will end so abruptly it'll feel like a death and it will put all the rest of your plans—for your family, for your career—on life support.

You will almost die, but you'll make it—just barely. Your survival won't have anything to do with your own abilities. You'll make it out alive completely because of the grit, sacrifice, and outright heroism of others. You haven't done anything to be worthy of their sacrifices, but these heroes will give you a second chance at life anyway.

Your second life begins when you wake up a few days later in agony. Nonstop, unrelenting, seemingly endless agony.

The pain is so all-consuming that you'll even tell the love of your life that you're going to shut down and be gone for a while to, quote, "circle the wagons." He'll be terrified because he thinks you're saying goodbye forever.

But you'll reemerge.

Sure, you'll be angry, vengeful, and scared, but most of all you'll dig into the deepest part of you and find a way to survive it. You'll realize how much you owe those around you and come out determined to never let them down and to live every day to repay them.

You'll be so grateful and proud not just of your husband,

who becomes your champion, but all those who sacrificed to keep you alive. You'll have to learn to walk, eat, bathe, and do everything again by falling, crawling, pulling yourself back up.

You'll remember that you are a soldier and that you will never give up, never abandon the mission, and as an officer it is your responsibility to take care of your troops. Because of that mission, you'll meet a powerful man, Senator Dick Durbin, who, instead of seeing someone pitiful and broken in a wheelchair, sees you as someone who can help make your nation better.

He'll challenge you to once again serve your nation, but this time by running for Congress. You will be apprehensive, but you'll say yes and work as hard as you can to succeed.

And you will fail. But this time, instead of just a personal failure like a bad grade or a swing and a strike, the world will know that you've failed. But somehow, it won't be as devastating as it would have been in your first life.

You'll pick yourself up again, because anything else would be to betray those who sacrificed to save you on that dusty field in Iraq. You'll reach, once again, into that well of gratitude to find a new way forward as an advocate for your fellow veterans.

And just a few years later, you'll find yourself in the best position you've ever been in to repay those who sacrificed to save you. You'll be a United States senator. People will start recognizing you. Strangers will stop you to say hello and to thank you for your work. You'll see the difference that you can make in people's lives. Your achievements now can actually make your nation a more perfect union.

And you'll be proud of it all, but as happy as you are to be able to help people, the best part of your second life will be you finally getting to have the family you've always wanted.

Senator Tammy Duckworth

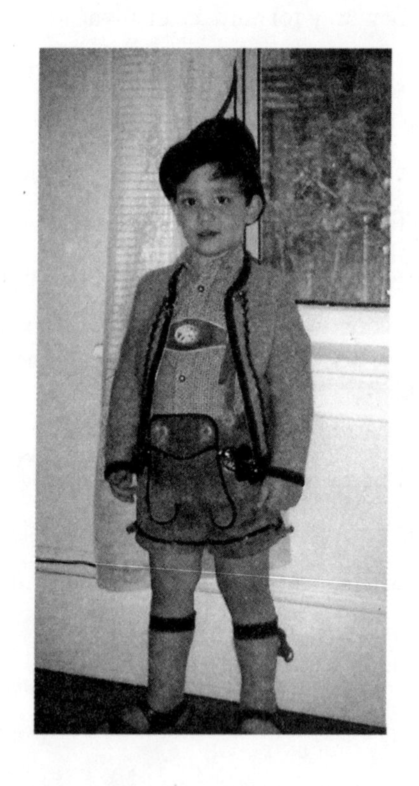

ALEXIS OHANIAN

Alexis Ohanian is an Armenian-American entrepreneur who cofounded Reddit, the third-largest website in the US. He and his wife, Serena Williams, have one daughter.

Alexis,

You're still a child and have no idea how much you'll enjoy laughing at that photo of you in lederhosen when you're older. Don't throw a fit; your mother and Oma, they really like it. You know how much you love mangoes? Well, you're surrounded by a small family with a simple life who loves you more than you love mangoes. They will give you confidence.

Your dad won't recognize the Brooklyn neighborhood you grew up in when you take him back to Fort Greene decades later. To fulfill your parents' dream of being able to afford to live in Brooklyn Heights, you'll buy an apartment there, though you'll end up living in Florida (and no, not Disney World).

You'll hate leaving NYC for the suburbs of Baltimore, but know that your parents are just doing what they think is best for your education with their limited means. Turns out they are right; you'll be bored, but you'll channel all that boredom into video games, and then computers, and eventually programming, which is going to be really helpful for later in life. You'll have to correct people who don't believe your name is Alexis all of your life . . . and you'll learn to love it.

You're making the right choice when you walk into the history department first semester of your first year at the University of Virginia to declare your major, shocking the department head at how early you commit. Trust your instincts. When you walk out of the LSAT without finishing it in order to go to the Waffle House, you're making the right choice. The decision is going to change your life. Because there between those syrupy bites of waffles, you're gonna realize that you're meant to be an entrepreneur, not a lawyer.

All those jobs you had growing up, from CompUSA sales guy to Pizza Hut cook, are going to help you tremendously when you cofound Reddit, but nothing can prepare you for your mom getting diagnosed with terminal brain cancer just a few months after graduating college and starting your company.

You're going to wish you could remember all the little details, her accented voice, her breathless laughter, the intensity of her hugs, and the charm of her high fives. She'll show you what it means to be truly courageous and selfless. And you'll spend the rest of your life working to make her sacrifices worth it. Let her hug and kiss you in public. It doesn't make you any less tough and it means everything to her. You'll understand when you're a father and you've got your own little *schatz.*

Speaking of dads, yours will show you what it means to be a man. He spent most of your childhood working late nights in order to provide for the family. And he'll support his wife throughout it all. He'll be an advocate through every chemo treatment and rock for her amid all the uncertainty, until the end. The whole ordeal gives you a wisdom at a young age—to realize what matters in life are the people and experiences, not things, one acquires along the way.

You'll have success in business, but there will be plenty of setbacks and surprises. Trust your instincts when it comes to people. Purge toxic relationships and spend time with the people who inspire you to be better. Start now. In fact, you'll be meeting some of your lifelong friends in elementary school very soon.

This is random, but bear with me. You'll do a class assignment in the fourth grade where you'll share just how much you hate tennis. That's fine for now, but promise me you'll keep an open mind later in life. You'll eventually get married, have a daughter, and even get your own mango tree. You'll spend your whole life creating websites, companies, even logos that millions of people love, but none of those compare to how proud of you are of your most important creation: your family.

Alexis

ALEX HONNOLD

Alex Honnold is an American free-solo rock climber. He became the first climber ever to free solo Yosemite's three-thousand-foot El Capitan wall.

Dear Alex,

Right now, you're an eighteen-year-old loner, lost in a sea of uncaring faces at UC Berkeley. You'll spend most of your freshman year not at class but at a local boulder, traversing the rock face back and forth with headphones in. You prefer it to the climbing gym because you don't have to talk to anyone. Surprisingly, this is the beginning of a path. You will leave school, move into a van, and devote yourself to climbing.

Your lack of social skills will be one part of why you take up free soloing, climbing by yourself without a rope. But don't worry—you'll eventually find yourself right at home in the climbing community, surrounded by close friends and lifelong partners.

You've always loved the physical movement of climbing. There's a certain joy in swinging around, propelling yourself upward, the fluidity of movement. Whether it's climbing trees or buildings as a kid or climbing Half Dome in Yosemite National Park as an adult, you'll come to appreciate the strain in your arms and the burning of your muscles. You'll experience this joy in climbing throughout your life; no matter how many routes you climb, it will always be at the core of your drive.

The idea of free soloing El Capitan, the iconic three-thousand-foot wall in Yosemite, will become an all-encompassing dream for much of your climbing life. For the first five or six years, you'll be too afraid to try—too afraid to even put any effort toward a potential solo. Right now, you're afraid of so many things: strangers, girls, vegetables, falling to your death. That's fine; fear is a perfectly natural part of life. You will always feel fear. But over time you will realize that the only way to truly manage your fears is to broaden your comfort zone. It's a long, slow process that requires constantly pushing yourself, but eventually you'll feel pretty darn good, and you'll climb big walls just like this.

You'll have near misses and frequently think about death. It will change your perspective and little annoyances will melt away. There will always be people calling you crazy or assuming that you have a death wish—that's fine. They don't see the amount of time and effort that goes into preparation or your drive to do something difficult, especially if it's never been done before. But you will always find purpose in exploring your own limits. Don't let anyone else's opinion rein you in. It doesn't matter what anyone else thinks: live your life in the way that you find most fulfilling.

For many years, climbing will be the most important thing in your life. You will put climbing before everything else. But keep an open mind. Eventually you will have a wonderful girlfriend and a charitable foundation.

In the end, it all comes back to El Capitan. It will give your life direction for almost a decade. It will be your muse, the reason you get up early to train and stay out for long days in the mountains. The day that you finally free solo El Cap will be one of the most satisfying of your life. It will also serve as an important reminder that no summit is more important than the long process of getting there.

Climbing is a lifelong journey; use it to learn and grow. And Alex, don't forget to enjoy the view.

Alex

We received a lot of feedback from the people on these pages that the experience of writing to your younger self is an emotional and healing process. So with that in mind, we've left a few blank pages here for you to write your own Note to Self. If you were inspired by some of the messages in these notes, know that it may be even more powerful to write one yourself!

—*Gayle*

NOTE TO SELF

NOTE TO SELF

NOTE TO SELF

NOTE TO SELF

NOTE TO SELF

NOTE TO SELF

NOTE TO SELF

NOTE TO SELF

NOTE TO SELF

NOTE TO SELF

NOTE TO SELF

Credits

1. Oprah: Courtesy of Oprah
2. Kermit the Frog: Copyright © Disney
3. Ryan O'Callaghan: Joe Robbins
4. Vice President Joe Biden: CBS Photo Archive
5. Kesha: Lagan Sebert/Courtesy of Shore Fire Media
6. Dale Earnhardt Jr.: Racing Photo Archives
7. Dr. Ruth: Maarten De Boer
8. Tyler Perry: Courtesy of Tyler Perry
9. Frank Gehry: Ralph Morse
10. Jane Fonda: Bettmann
11. John Lewis: Steve Schapiro
12. Alice Waters: Susan Wood/Getty Images

13. Scott Ostrom: Craig F. Walker
14. Piper Kerman: Christopher Lane
15. Chris Rosati: Courtesy of Anna Rosati
16. Peggy Whitson: Courtesy of Peggy Whitson
17. Taya Kyle: Courtesy of Taya Kyle
18. President Jimmy Carter: PhotoQuest
19. Danica Patrick: Jared C. Tilton
20. Art Garfunkel: CBS Photo Archive
21. Jimmy Greene: Anthony Pidgeon
22. Tim Howard: Ashley Allen
23. Chelsea Handler: Courtesy of Chelsea Handler
24. Chris Herren: Courtesy of Chris Herren
25. Jim McGreevey: Courtesy of Jim McGreevey
26. Dr. Maya Angelou: Michael Ochs Archives/Getty Images

27: Tracy Morgan: Courtesy of Tracy Morgan

28: Heather Duckworth: Courtesy of Heather Duckworth

29: Adam Rippon: Courtesy of Adam Rippon

30: François Clemmons: Courtesy of François Clemmons

31: Tammy Duckworth: Courtesy of Tammy Duckworth

32: Alexis Ohanian: Courtesy of Alexis Ohanian

33: Alex Honnold: Courtesy of Dierdre Wolownick